INFINITY'S ILLUSTRATED CLASSICS

The Invisible Man

H. G. WELLS

Retold by W. Sequeira & A. D' Souza and Re-illustrated.

INFINITY BOOKS

THE INVISIBLE MAN

ISBN 81-7929-225-8

First Edition of 18 Titles 2001, Reprinted 2002, 2003, 2004 (Twice), 2005 (For export), 2006, 2007, 2008. This title added to the series in 2010 Reprinted 2011, 2012, 2013 & 2014 (Special Edition), 2015, 2016, 2017.

Published for:

ADARSH ENTERPRISES

4393/4 Tulsidas Street, Ansari Road,
Darya Ganj, New Delhi-110002
Phones: 23246131, 23246132. Fax: 011-23246130.
Email: adarshbooks@vsnl.com

Printed at : Saurabh Printers Pvt. Ltd.

Contents

CHAPTER	PAGE
1. The Arrival of a Bandaged Stranger	5
2. Starting an Experiment	18
3. Nothing Could Be Seen!	28
4. A Strange Robbery	40
5. Removing the Bandages	46
6. Escape of the Invisible Man	60
7. Meeting the Invisible Man	70
8. Destruction in Iping	80
9. Finding an Accomplice	91
10. The Rampage at Jolly Cricketer Inn	100
11. A Mysterious Visitor	111
12. An Amazing Discovery	128
13. The Invisible Man Tells His Story	138
14. A Threat	152
15. Mr. Kemp's Visitor Escapes	164

Contents

CHAPTER PAGE

16. An Attempt To Trace The Invisible Man 170

17. The Assault at Kemp's House 178

18. The End of Terror 191

19. The Invisible Man Inn 198

THE ARRIVAL OF A BANDAGED STRANGER

On a cold snowy night in February, a stranger alighted from the train at Bramblehurst railway station, in the southern part of England. He was fully covered from head to toe in a large-brimmed hat and a long black overcoat. His hands were covered with gloves as well. But they could hardly guard him against the biting February wind and the snow, which piled on

The arrival of a mysterious stranger

him and also on the black suitcase that he was carrying.

No carriages could be seen at the station and the man had to struggle a lot, as he had to make his way through the storm for many hours, before he could finally reach the small village of Iping.

He was almost half-dead when he reached his destination. He flung open the door of the Coach and Horses Inn, totally exhausted by the journey. He kept his head down on his chest and somehow managed to say, "Please arrange for a room and fire fast!"

"Welcome sir! I'm Mrs. Hall, the innkeeper here," a woman said as she appeared from behind the bar. "I shall take you to your room, sir. Kindly follow me upstairs."

The stranger turned his back towards

Mrs. Hall as they talked about the charges of the room and food. Mrs. Hall lighted a fire in the fireplace and then went downstairs for preparing food for him.

When Mrs. Hall returned with a tray of freshly prepared hot meal, the room was already warm and comfortable because of the fire. She found the stranger standing at the window looking out at the storm. He was still wearing his coat, hat and gloves.

"Can I take your coat and hat sir?" asked Mrs. Hall. "I shall dry them in the kitchen as the snow is melting down from them on my carpet."

"There is no need," the man said sharply as he faced Mrs. Hall. "I don't want to take them off."

At that time Mrs. Hall got the chance to see the man's face properly for the first time.

Mrs Hall saw his face for the first time

Right below his wide-brimmed hat, were big blue glasses that completely covered his eyes from the front and sides. His cheeks and chin were also completely covered by thick beard and sideburns that touched the collar of his coat.

"Okay sir! No problem," Mrs. Hall said as she left the room.

After getting back to the kitchen Mrs. Hall realized that she had served meat to the man without the mustard. So she went upstairs with the mustard.

She knocked the door once and then opened it. The man was taken aback by seeing her suddenly. He quickly crouched down under the table and Mrs. Hall could see nothing but a flash of white.

Seeing the hat and the overcoat lying on a chair, Mrs. Hall asked, "Can I take these with me now, sir?"

"Yes you can take the coat but don't take the hat," the man said in a dull voice while sitting up.

Mrs. Hall was wide-eyed with shock at what she saw in front of her. The man's head was wrapped in white bandages and only a shiny pink nose was visible. Thick patches of black hair could be seen here and there between the bandages. His hands were also equally strange. They were still gloved and held a large napkin that concealed his mouth and jaw. He was wearing a dark brown dressing gown with its collar turned up and the front part was covered with a scarf. "Don't take the hat," the man said again.

"A-all right sir!" Mrs. Hall stammered still in a state of shock. "It was not known to me, sir, that..."

"That's all for now, madam. Thank you."

The bandages scare Mrs Hall

"The poor man must have had an accident or surgery," Mrs. Hall mumbled to herself as she hurriedly left the room and shut the door behind her, shivering.

"Those bandages scared me like anything. And it must be painful for him to talk with an injured mouth like that. That's why he must have kept his mouth covered with the napkin. Poor man!"

After finishing his meal, the stranger sat in an armchair in front of the fireplace and lit his pipe. He covered the lower part of his face with the scarf knowing that Mrs. Hall would come back for the tray. He left just a small space open near his lips for the pipe.

On entering the man's room Mrs. Hall felt that the food, the drink and the fire had made his attitude a little gentle. He spoke with Mrs. Hall more cordially than before.

"Mrs. Hall, my luggage is at Bramblehurst station. Can you arrange to bring it here?"

"My husband will be coming back late tonight with our horse and cart. I shall ask him to get the luggage tomorrow."

"Can't someone else go to the station tonight?"

"No, because the roads are steep and chances of meeting with accidents are very high tonight because of the rough weather. I am sure you can understand how dangerous accidents can..."

"Yes Mrs. Hall! I do understand. I had an accident as well. My eyes have become weak ever since and I am bound to stay in darkness, wearing these big glasses most of the time."

"What exactly happened, may I..."

"That is really not important madam. But for now, let me tell you that I am a scientist and I am working on a very important experiment. All my books, instruments, chemicals and notes are in my baggage. I must start my work as soon as possible. But if I can't get the luggage before tomorrow, it will have to do. Goodnight, Mrs. Hall."

"Poor man! No wonder he's so sensitive about accidents," Mrs. Hall murmured to herself as she left the room.

She hastily went downstairs to the bar and gave a vivid description of her mysterious guest to her customers.

Everybody expressed their sympathy on hearing about the accident except Teddy Henfrey, the village clockmaker.

"I don't believe that he has had an accident," said Teddy. "I think he is hiding from the police and that's the reason he has wrapped himself up in bandages."

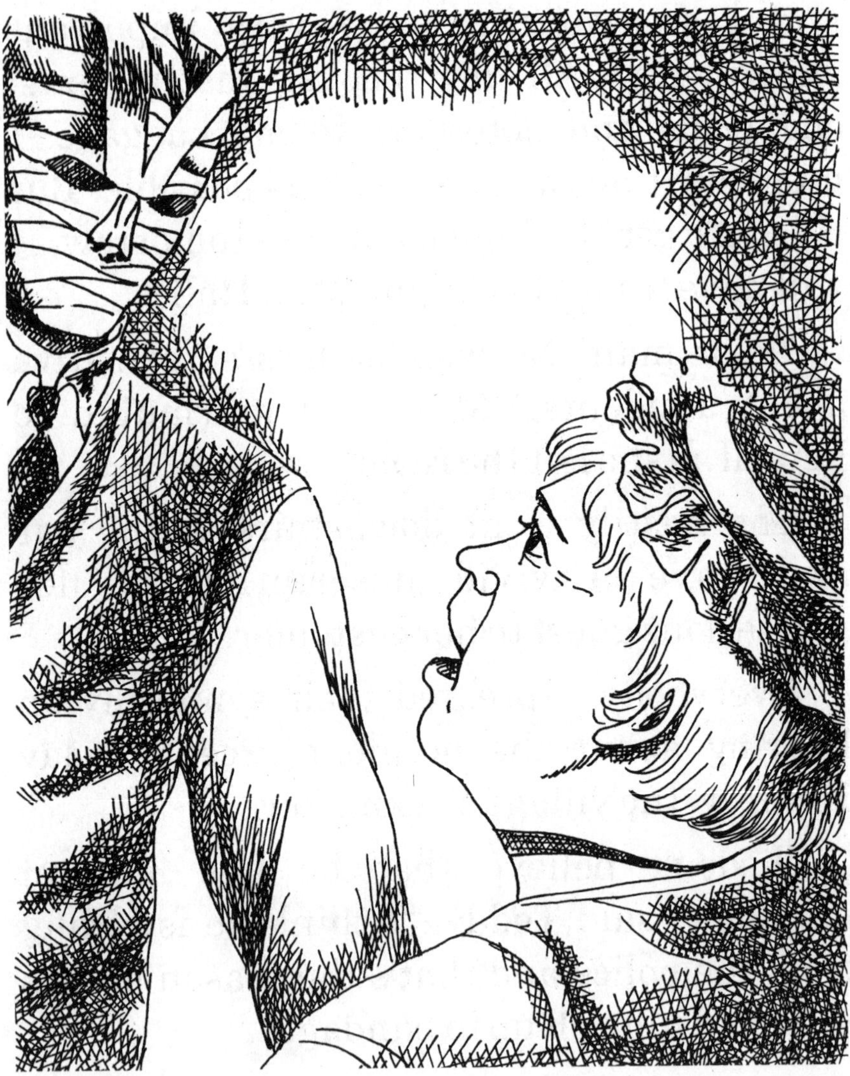

Mrs Hall was suspicious of the strange guest

"May I know who's hiding and what bandages are you talking about?" said a voice at the inn's door.

"It's the strange guest, whom your wife just rented a room to, Mr. Hall," Teddy replied. "I would surely check his luggage after you get it from the station tomorrow."

"Teddy, would you please mind your own business?" Mrs. Hall shouted. "And Hall, you too please don't interfere. This is my inn and I will do whatever I feel is correct!"

Even though Mrs. Hall said those strong words, she could not deny to herself that the strange guest was indeed suspicious. That night her dreams were filled with those suspicions. She dreamt of white turnip heads with big black eyes, at the end of long necks... and those heads were chasing her everywhere she went!

STARTING AN EXPERIMENT

The following morning, Mrs. Hall drove his cart up to the inn and called out for help to take off the mysterious man's luggage.

"Oh my God!" exclaimed Mrs. Hall as she came out. "I had expected only a few trunks to be put in his room, but here I see dozens of boxes, six wooden crates. I wonder what else is there in the luggage!"

"Please come fast along with my luggage," said the stranger as he came out of the inn. "I waited for a long time for those things." The collar of his coat was turned up, his wide-brimmed hat was pulled down to cover his face and his dark gloves covered his hands.

The stranger was just about to lift one small crate from the cart when a neighborhood dog came running and leapt at his hand. Mr. Hall tried to reach into the cart for his whip, but the dog's teeth left the man's gloved hand and bit his trouser leg.

The next moment, Mr. Hall beat the dog's back with his whip. The dog was forced to release his bite on the man's trousers. Mr. Hall cursed and shouted at the dog's owner and the stranger glancing at his torn glove and trousers quickly went back to his room.

"Let me go and see if he is all right," said Mr. Hall.

"Yes, please go. Fast," said his wife.

The man's coat arm had no hand in it.

The stranger's door was open. Hall entered the room to sympathize with the man and to offer any help that the stranger might need. The room was dark with the curtains closed, and Hall was shocked at what he saw–the man was waving his coat's arm at him... but without a hand! Before Hall could understand anything, he was hit hard in the chest and then pushed out of the room. Then the door slammed in his face. Hall was baffled and he stood outside the room scratching his head. "What was that? Did I see anything at all?"

He then went back downstairs, still bemused and found that there was a crowd in front of the inn as Mrs. Hall was arguing with the dog's owner, who was holding the dog by its collar.

Hall was still confused at what had happened in the man's room. He told Mrs. Hall, "I offered help but he didn't want any.

Let's get his luggage up to him."

"You must get a doctor to have a look at the bite," said a woman in the crowd.

"But I didn't see any blood. And when the gloves and the trouser tore, I didn't see any skin either," said another.

"Whatever it may be," said a man. "Just shoot the dog and end the matter here."

Just then, the dog tried to drift away and pointing his nose towards the inn began to gnarl. Everyone looked at the entrance.

"Come along, Mr. Hall," said the stranger in an angry voice. He was wearing new trousers and fresh pair of gloves. He had his coat's collar turned up as before and his hat was pulled down to cover his face. "Did you get hurt, sir?" asked Mrs. Hall.

"Not at all. The dog didn't bite the skin. Can you please hurry up with those things, Mr. Hall?"

He moved the test tubes around

As soon as the crates had been set down in the stranger's room he desperately jumped at them and began unpacking. He littered straws from the crates everywhere in the room and on the carpet as he started taking out various instruments and books filled with handwritten notes. There were millions of test tubes and bottles of different shapes, sizes and colors containing powders, fluids and some were labeled Poison. He put them up all over the room, on cabinets, shelves, bookcases, window sills and tables and the room looked quite like a village pharmacy than a bedroom.

Soon after the man began with his experiment and the trunks of clothes and books were left untouched. All morning he kept working. He poured drops of liquids from the bottles into test tubes and mixed and swooshed them with different powders. Mrs. Hall walked inside his room with the lunch tray but he didn't stop even then.

He didn't pay any attention to her and as she put his tray on the table she looked up to see that the man was not wearing his glasses.

"Oh my God!" Mrs. Hall gasped under her breath at the sight. "His eye sockets look empty!"

The stranger heard her gasp and hurriedly wore his glasses. "I don't know how you could enter without knocking!" he snarled.

"Sir, I knocked for quite sometime... but you didn't hear..."

"Okay! May be you knocked. But my experiment is very important to me and it demands full attention. I don't want any disturbance from now on."

"I absolutely understand, sir. And there is also a lock at the door which you can use whenever you want. And sir, these heaps of straw scattered all over the room would mean extra clean..."

The strange guest asks not to be bothered

"Fine! Just put an extra charge on my bill. And I will be highly grateful if you don't bother me with these trivial things. Kindly let me work now!" The next several hours were quiet as the stranger worked in silence. Then suddenly Mrs. Hall was astonished to hear the sounds of smashing bottles and also rapid footsteps moving all over the room. Mrs. Hall ran up the stairs thinking something dreadful must have happened. She tried to listen at the door, too scared to knock.

"It's impossible for me to go on like this!"She heard the man speak in anger. "I can't continue with this anymore! All my life will be spent in getting the result of this experiment! I neither have much time nor do I have the patience to finish off this experiment! What can I do?"

NOTHING COULD BE SEEN!

The stranger worked steadily for the next two months, till the end of April. He took breaks very rarely to go for walks, but only at twilight.

He always kept his hands and face concealed in covers whenever he went out or Mrs. Hall came to his room with his meal. On his walks he never responded to the greetings of the villagers and he enjoyed scaring the children who tried to tease him. He kept his door locked and talked to himself angrily and kept on smashing furniture and his devices.

Whenever Mrs. Hall complained to him about her ruined and broken furnishings, he always made an extra payment to compensate for the loss. Several times Mr. Hall asked his wife to get rid of the stranger but every time Mrs. Hall told him, “There are not many guests in this inn. Let’s wait till summer. For now we can use the money that he is paying us.”

The stranger became a regular topic of discussion during his three months in Iping. Whenever Mrs. Hall faced a question regarding the stranger she gave explanations like, “He is a scientist and works for the government. Currently he is busy with a secret project,” or “He avoids coming out in the public since he had a very bad accident which

They thought he was a criminal

damaged and bruised his face and hands badly."

Most of the villagers believed what Teddy Henfrey said, that the man was a criminal and he kept himself wrapped up in bandages only because he was hiding from the police. The rest of the people did not bother much and thought that he was a harmless mad person.

There was one person in Iping who was very curious to find out more about the stranger. His name was John Cuss. He was the village doctor and was fascinated by the stories of the "thousands" of bottles in the man's room and wanted to see them. He finally thought of an excuse to visit the stranger a request for a donation for the Iping Nurse Fund and went to the Coach and Horses Inn.

Mrs. Hall took the doctor upstairs and

knocked at the stranger's room. They heard a low voice muttering something and thinking it to be the permission to enter the room they opened the door and went inside.

Mrs. Hall didn't leave the hallway after Mr. Cuss went inside the room because she was too curious to hear their conversation. She stood there for ten minutes but could not hear anything other than murmurs.

Then suddenly she heard a sharp cry, a ruffling of feet and a wild laughter which made her jump in surprise.

Then flinging the door open Dr. Cuss came running out of the room with a pale white face, totally scared. He almost knocked Mrs. Hall down while rushing down the stairs. Then he ran out of the door.

Mrs. Hall heard the stranger's wild laughter and then the door of his room closed with a bang.

Mr Cuss ran as fast as he could

Mr. Cuss ran as fast as he could and went to Reverend Bunting's house. The churchman was in his study when the doctor came running to him and gasped, "I am sure I have become insane. Do I look as if I have lost my mind?"

The reverend was taken aback by this and he looked up from the sermon that he was writing. "Insane? What are you talking about Cuss?" The doctor was out of breath and somehow managed to say, "It's the mysterious man at the inn. He is so scary and I just had the most frightening experience of my life with him. I went to meet him to collect donation for the Nurse Fund. As soon as I opened the door he hurriedly hid his hands inside his pockets and slouched down in his chair. While talking with him about the donation I kept on looking at the bottles, chemicals, powders and test tubes scattered everywhere in the room. And then I directly asked him, 'Are you researching on a secret experiment?'

"He had caught a bad cold and in between his sneezes he barked at me, 'If you must know, yes I am working on a secret experiment! After long years of research and study I have found the answer for well you need not know what! I had written all the ingredients on a sheet of paper and kept it on my table, when a breeze from the open window blew it towards the fireplace. It was carried up the chimney and I rushed to grab it by reaching out my arm like this -"

"And he took out his arm before me to show how he had tried to reach out to get the paper. But I was shocked to see that there was no hand and the sleeve was empty! Seeing that, I thought may be he had an artificial arm and had taken it off for some

The missing arm

reason. But then I wondered, how could he keep his sleeve up without an arm? I looked right through the sleeve but there was no arm! I found him staring -"

"Yes... Then what happened? Go on."

"That's all. He didn't say anything. He stared at me angrily and then put his sleeve back inside his pocket. And then just as he was about to return to the story of the paper, I asked him directly, 'How could you do that... I mean move an empty sleeve?'

"Then he stood up and walked towards me till he was just a few inches away from me. His bandaged face and those uncanny glasses gave me the creeps."

"Then he asked me in an evil voice, 'Did you say my sleeve was empty?" "Yes! Of course I did."

"Then again he pulled out his sleeve from

his pocket and tried to show it to me again. I was bewildered to see an empty sleeve approaching me and had a strange creepy feeling. Then suddenly I felt as if a finger and a thumb - pinched my nose."

The reverend laughed loudly hearing this.

"Oh don't laugh! You really don't know how I felt to see that there was no arm in the sleeve!" said Cuss in a frightened voice.

Reverend Bunting shook his head in disbelief and thought that either the old doctor had imagined all that or may be he had taken to drinking. "Oh Reverend, please believe me!" pleaded the doctor. "I swayed my arm at him and hit his sleeve... and I felt that there was an arm, but I could not see it! Something could be felt, but nothing could be seen! Nothing, I tell you! Nothing! It was as if he was a ghost wearing clothes!"

The Reverend's wife woke him

A STRANGE ROBBERY

A few weeks later, at the end of May, a strange robbery took place at Reverend Bunting's home. One morning, just before dawn, Mrs. Bunting woke up from her sleep hearing the sound of soft footsteps. It seemed as if someone was walking barefooted outside the bedroom and down the staircase.

"Mr. Bunting, wake up!" Mrs. Bunting said softly to her sleeping husband. "There's someone in the house!"

The reverend woke up. After putting on his spectacles and slippers he wrapped Mrs. Bunting's dressing gown around him and took a poker from the fireplace as a protection from any attack. Then he stood at the top of the staircase, to listen. He heard sounds of violent sneeze coming from his study downstairs.

He went downstairs to his study with his wife closely behind him, in the dark. There was absolute silence except for the slight creaking of the stair and occasional odd sniffles and rustling of papers in the study. When they got to the end of the stairs there was silence again.

They found the door of the study ajar and peeked inside. Reverend Bunting had left the room absolutely dark the night before but now the room was illuminated by a candle, which was placed on the desk. There was no sign of the robber but the drawer in the room was open.

Suddenly the sound of the clinking of coins broke the silence.

"The robber has found our housekeeping money," whispered Mrs. Bunting. "I had kept more than two pounds in gold sovereigns in the drawer." Hearing this, the reverend got into action. He went inside the room with the poker in his hand and shouted fiercely, "Who's there? I have caught you! Come out and surrender!"

Then Reverend Bunting stopped so suddenly that Mrs. Bunting crashed into him.

"But the room is empty! There's nobody here!" he exclaimed looking around in surprise.

"But I'm certain that there's someone in here," Mrs. Bunting claimed.

The Buntings stood there dumbfounded for a while and then began searching the room. They tried to find the robber under the desk, behind the curtains, out of the window, up the chimney and also inside the wastepaper basket and coal scuttle but found nobody.

"How's this possible?" said the reverend, shocked. "Nobody's here! But this candle is lit up! Strange!"

"Mr. Bunting, just have a look at the drawer! It's open and the money's stolen," cried the puzzled Mrs. Bunting.

"A-CHOO!" Suddenly a big sneeze could be heard at the hallway.

Mr. Bunting and his wife came running out of the study but they had to stop by the loud slamming of the kitchen door. They were panting heavily but still ran to the

"Let's go to the cellar"

kitchen and opened the door. But only an empty garden could be seen in the faint light of dawn.

"Let's go to the cellar!" cried the reverend. "Follow me with a candle, fast!" The Buntings searched desperately every inch of the cellar and also the cabinet and pantry in the kitchen. But nobody could be found there. Then they went for a thorough search in every room of their house. The candle burned down in Mrs. Bunting's hand, yet they could not find the robber and they were as confused as when they had first found the candle lit up in the desk of the study.

REMOVING THE BANDAGES

At six o' clock on the same morning of the puzzling robbery at Reverend Bunting's place, Mrs. Hall found the bolts on the front door of the inn had been slid back and the door was slightly open.

"How come the door is open? I had locked it myself last night, before going to bed!" exclaimed Mrs. Hall. "Who could..."

"Must be the mad scientist!" said Mr. Hall

pointing up at the stranger's room. "Come, let's check!"

While going upstairs Mr. Hall heard the sound of coughing and thought that it was from his wife in front of him. Mrs. Hall heard the same cough and thought that it was from Mr. Hall, behind her.

They reached in front of the stranger's room and knocked at his door but nobody replied.

"See if the door is locked or not," said Mrs. Hall.

Mr. Hall turned the knob and the door opened easily.

"Just have a look! The bed is empty and there's no one in the room! Where is he?" he whispered.

But Mrs. Hall stood there petrified staring at the big armchair near the fireplace.

"Look!" she blurted out. "His coat, trousers, shoes and glasses are lying on the chair! And there's his hat... hanging on top of the bed post!"

"And look... He has removed his bandages also! They are heaped on the table!" said Mr. Hall in amazement. "All his clothes and bandages are here, but he's not."

"This is really strange!" said Mrs. Hall as she went near the bed. She touched the pillow and the bed sheet and said, "These are cold. He must be out for more than an hour!"

Just at that moment, something weird and uncanny happened. The sheets and blankets piled themselves up in a heap and leaped up into a peak, then jumped on the floor! The stranger's hat hopped off the bedpost and whirled through the air into Mrs. Hall's face! The very next moment they heard a thunderous laughter in that room. The

The man was nowhere to be found

armchair turned itself on its side and threw the coat, trousers, shoes and glasses on the floor. Then it came flying through the air towards Mrs. Hall.

Mrs. Hall screamed and looked at her husband frightfully. The chair slowed itself a bit and then rested itself against her back. And the next moment it pushed the husband and the wife out of the room.

The door closed loudly and the lock snapped shut. Then everything was silent again.

Mrs. Hall almost became unconscious against her husband. She said, "It can't be anything other than evil spirit! I'm certain of it."

"Jenny please calm down," said Mr. Hall. "There has to be an explanation. Let's go downstairs now."

The Halls screamed and ran

Once Mrs. Hall steadied herself after drinking a cup of tea, she told Mr. Hall, "George, we have to get rid of the man somehow. Did you see how he's put evil spirits into the furniture in his room?"

"What rubbish are you talking about my room?" came a menacing voice from the staircase.

Mr. and Mrs. Hall looked up fearfully and saw that it was the stranger standing there in his clothes, glasses and gloves. He had also wrapped himself in bandages like before. He gave them a dirty look and said, "Why did you get into my room without my permission? Can't you both just leave me alone?" Saying that he went upstairs in a fury and locked the door.

"W-we just went up to his room, but he wasn't there! How did he know we were there in his room and how could he come down now," gasped Mrs. Hall.

Mr. Hall was so puzzled that he could only shake his head in reply. For the next six hours none of them went near his room. Mrs. Hall didn't even answer the bell when the stranger rang it. "I think he wants his meal. But he can easily go to the devil for that!" she told her husband in an angry voice.

The bar was almost full by noon. The usual customers came there and everyone talked about the mysterious robbery that took place at the reverend's house. But the discussion stopped suddenly when the stranger, in his gloves, hat and long coat stepped into the bar.

He stared at Mrs. Hall and demanded, "Why didn't I get my breakfast? And why didn't you answer my bell?"

"May I know why haven't you paid your bill yet?" Mrs. Hall asked rudely. "I gave you the bill five days back!"

Demanding his breakfast

"I had informed you already that I have spent all my money and was expecting it in the mail by today," he snapped back.

"Well I'm sorry to say that if you don't pay the bill, you will neither get food nor the room."

Realizing that he was at Mrs. Hall's mercy, the stranger softened his voice and said politely, "But I have the money now."

"Really? May I ask where did you suddenly get the money from?" Mrs. Hall demanded, remembering the discussion at the bar about the robbery at the reverend's house. "You have to give me certain explanations also. What have you done to my chair upstairs? And we found your room empty at six o' clock this morning. So how did you get into the room? You didn't enter by the door like the other guests! I'm sure."

Hearing this the stranger stamped his foot in anger and raised his gloved hand. “Enough!” he said fiercely.

Mrs. Hall backed away and didn't utter a single word.

“You can’t understand who or what I am,” he said in an unnerving calmness. “But don’t worry! By Heaven, I’ll show you!” So saying he put his hand in front of his face and then withdrew it.

And only a black hole could be seen where his nose had been. “Here, see this,” he said taking Mrs. Hall’s hand and placed something rubbery and soft in her palm.

The woman looked down at her palm in bewilderment. And then she realized what the stranger had placed in her palm. She stepped back in shock and dropped in on the floor, trembling in fear, “A nose! He's taken off his nose!”

He placed his nose in her hand

The stranger ignored what she said and the cries from the villagers at the bar. With his gloved hand he took off his hat and removed his blue glasses.

Then he tore off his ugly whiskers and patches of hair violently, and started taking off the bandages from his head.

The villagers stood there horrified. They could not believe what they saw in front of them. They thought that they would see a distorted, bruised, ugly face.... something atrocious. But they were not prepared to see nothing!

Mrs. Hall screamed hysterically as she moved back and ran towards the door. Everyone in the room followed her and knocked over each other in fear.

The only man who remained unmoved

inside the Coach and Horses Inn was a figure dressed in gloves, trousers and long coat with its collar turned up. But above the collar there was nothing, nothing at all!

ESCAPE OF THE INVISIBLE MAN

The villagers in Iping heard screams and cries coming from the men who were running away from the bar. But the curious villagers started running towards the inn, to find out what the excitement was all about. Mrs. Hall after escaping from the inn collapsed in Mr. Hall's arms, and the crowd tried to explain the weird happenings.

"The man didn't have a head!"

"He must be a magician. It was a trick."

"It must be an evil spirit sent by the devil!"

"Stop everybody!" a voice called from the back of the crowd. It was Mr. Jaffers, the village constable.

"He's right there, inside the inn. The man without a head!" cried Mr. Hall. "Well, with head or without head, Hall, I've come to take him behind the bars."

Hall took the constable inside the inn and up to the man's room. He flung the door open and said, 'Go ahead constable. Please do your duty." Jaffers marched in, with Hall behind him.

"That's the man we were talking about," said Hall, as he pointed to the headless figure. The Invisible Man was holding a piece of bread and a lump of cheese in his gloved hands.

The arrest of a headless man

"What's going on?" an angry voice demanded from the empty space above the collar.

"I've come to arrest you, head or headless," said Jaffers.

"If you stay away from me, it will be better for you," warned the figure, stepping back from Jaffers.

All of a sudden, the food dropped. The stranger's glove came across Jaffer's face and slapped him hard. The constable managed to catch the handless left wrist and clutched the invisible throat.

The Invisible Man kicked the constable hard on his leg but he did not give in. The two men clutched and hit each other and then both fell down on the floor.

"Hold him by the feet!" shouted the constable.

As Hall tried to grab the stranger's feet, he was kicked hard in his ribs and he crashed against his wife's favorite closet.

Jaffers somehow managed to get on top of the headless man but he soon found himself rolling over on his back.

The Invisible Man stood up over Jaffers and calmly said, "I give in!" Then he took off his right glove.

With his invisible hands the stranger quickly opened the buttons along the front of his jacket. Then the jacket and trousers stooped over and fumbled with the shoes and socks.

Standing above the stooped-over stranger, Hall gasped, "He's not a human being at all! Look inside his collar and clothes. There's nothing inside!" Then he tried to push his hand into the emptiness and suddenly pulled it back with a cry of pain.

The man became invisible

"I'd be grateful if you keep your fingers out)f my eyes," said the man from somewhere ıbove his clothes. "I'm all here, with heads, ıands and all parts of my body. Yes, I'm nvisible but that doesn't give anyone the ·ight to poke me to bits or to arrest me!"

By now, several villagers had crowded nside the room. The constable declared, "I'm ıere to arrest you on charges of breaking into ı house and stealing money. And for that I'll ıandcuff you too."

"Nonsense!" cried the man. "I'll go with ou to prove that I'm not a thief or a robber. 3ut I'll never allow you to handcuff me!"

"But I've to follow my proper procedures ınd orders," declared the constable. ;uddenly the Invisible Man sat down and ›efore anyone could understand what he was loing, he took off his shoes and socks and pulled down his trousers. The jacket began shaking loosely from the shirt underneath when the constable suddenly realized what the Invisible Man was trying to do.

"Stop!" he ordered. And as he tried to pull at the jacket it slid off in his hands. "Hold him!" he cried to others. "It will be impossible to find him, if he takes off his shirt too!"

But just after that, a fluttering white shirt was moving here and there in the room. It came near Hall and gave him a hard blow in his face.

Then it lifted itself up, as if it was being pulled over a man's head. Jaffers tried to stop it but succeeded only in helping to take it off. In answer, a hard fist smashed his mouth.

By now, there was a hurricane inside the room. People hit each other's faces or heads in confusion. Cries of "Grab him!" and "Don't let him escape!" filled the room. The furious

A white shirt flew through the room

swinging and hitting continued which caused bloody noses, black eyes, broken tooth and smashed jaws.

Suddenly the constable shouted, “I’ve got him!”

The confused mob started coming out in the hallway as Jaffers pushed his way through, holding the invisible prisoner tightly. Then a hard kick smashed his knees and he crouched down on the floor loosening his hold on the Invisible Man. He was then pushed down the steps and his head was banged against the hard stone on the floor, where he lay bleeding and unconscious.

A woman standing on the doorway of the inn felt something push her aside. Something kicked the dog on the road and it growled. An old man was thrown off his bicycle into a ditch by an invisible force.

The Invisible Man escaped!

MEETING THE INVISIBLE MAN

Almost one and a half mile out of the village of Iping, a tramp was sitting in a ditch at the side of the road. His feet were without shoes. His name was Thomas Marvel. He had two pairs of shoes in front of him, both charity gifts. The man was confused, because he was unable to decide which pair to wear. One was too large for him by about four sizes, while the soles of the other pair were too flimsy to wear in clammy weather.

Marvel's head was covered with a fringed silk hat and it tilted on his crinkled and rough face as he looked up at the sky. He was wondering whether it would be a dry breezy day or there would be a spring rain before evening. Hours ago, when he sat down in the ditch, he had loosened the coat that was covering his short, plump figure. And now as he was busy studying his boots, he wore the coat properly by tying the twine that held the coat together in places, where there used be buttons once.

Suddenly he heard a voice behind him, which disturbed his concentration, "Both the boots are too ugly to wear."

"Correct," he consented without looking back. "But it's difficult to decide which one is uglier. What boots are ye wearin'?" And he turned his head over his shoulder to watch the speaker's boots.

Hearing a voice speak from nowhere

But he was surprised to see that there were neither boots nor legs nor any man standing behind him. Then he looked at the other side but nobody was there either.

The tramp got down on all fours and crawled in circle to find the speaker. But he could not see anyone, "Where are ye hiding?" he exclaimed.

"I think I was talking to myself! Am I drunk?" he said to himself scratching his long thick beard.

"Relax!" You're not drunk!" he heard the voice again.

"Are ye a ventriloquist? Or are ye buried here in the ground?"

"I'm not what you think, my friend!"

The tramp stood up and turned himself to look around several times, "I'm sure I heard a voice speaking' to me!"

"Yes, you obviously did hear me!"

Suddenly Marvel felt that he was grabbed by the collar and shaken vigorously.

"I worried so much about these silly boots that I'm losing my mind. Or is it some evil spirit?"

"Neither have you gone mad nor am I an evil spirit."

"Then my mind is playing tricks."

"Well, I'm going to throw some pebbles at you. See if it's your imagination or the reality." And from a little distance away from where he was standing, came a volley of stones at him. Some hit him at his shoulder, while others fell at his feet in the ditch.

"Are you imagining this also?" said the voice.

Marvel sat down in amazement. "How can these stones move by themselves? How can they talk?"

"Simple. It's not the stones, it's me. I'm invisible."

"Of course ye are! Ye needn't tell me that. But why are ye hiding'?"

"I'm not hiding. It's just that you can't see me because I'm invisible. I'm standing just a few feet away from you."

"Come on! I'm not a fool. May be I'm a tramp but I'm not mad or ignorant. How can ye be as thin as the air?"

"I am. You can look through me because I'm invisible. I'm a human being and I too need food, drink and clothes."

"Then let me take your hand and find out Lord! Ye made me jump holding my hand so tightly!"

The tramp touched the hand that held his wrist. And then he touched an invisible muscular arm, an invisible throbbing chest

Feeling the Invisible Man

and an invisible bearded face.

"This is unbelievable!" he cried. " I can see a rabbit running across the field through ye!" Then he looked at the invisible stomach more intently and asked with a little hesitation, "Did ye eat bread and cheese some time back?"

"Yes! I ate them a while ago. You can see them because my system hasn't yet digested them totally."

"Amazing'! Are ye a magician?"

"No. It's a long story and I will tell you later about it. For now, I need help. I'm roaming around the countryside without clothes. When I saw you sitting in the ditch I thought you are just like me, lonely and outcasted by the society. Perhaps you would want to travel with me and help me."

"How may I help ye, Mr. Invisible?"

Seeing the food inside the Invisible Man

"I need shelter and clothes first. I shall tell you later what else I need."

"Look, I'm just an ignorant tramp. How can I be of any help to ye? Please let me go!" Marvel pleaded as he tried to back off from the voice.

"No! You should help me. Of all people in Iping I've chosen you. If you help me now, I'll do great things for you later. Just imagine what power I have. I'm invisible!"

The voice paused and then a violent sneeze could be heard. Then it threatened, "If you don't help me or follow my orders -"

Marvel felt a tap on his shoulder and he jumped in fear. "How can I betray ye? I will help ye in whichever way I can. But please don't harm me Mr. Invisible Man."

DESTRUCTION IN IPING

By afternoon, Iping became peaceful as before. The people who believed that the Invisible Man existed were relieved that he had left Iping, and those who doubted in his existence made jokes about what had happened at the Coach and Horses Inn that morning.

Around four o' clock that day it was noticed that a tramp had entered the village.

He was short and plump. He seemed to be restless and upset. It was seen that he was talking to himself as he walked hurriedly towards the Coach and Horses Inn.

Mr. Thomas Marvel chose to ignore the men sitting at the bar and he headed directly to the room of the Invisible Man. When he opened the door he saw Dr. Cuss and Reverend Bunting were sitting at the desk examining three thick notebooks each titled "Diary".

"It's written in code language," said the doctor.

"Or may be we don't know this strange language..." said the reverend.

"There,"said a voice at the door.

Both Dr. Cuss and the reverend looked up horrified, thinking that the Invisible Man had returned. But seeing a tramp with rosy

They call Marvel to the bar downstairs

cheeks, they both breathed a sigh of relief and smiled.

"The bar is downstairs, my dear man," said the doctor.

"Thank ye," said Marvel and went downstairs. He had a drink at the bar and then went out of the inn. He looked around cautiously and after becoming sure that nobody was watching, he briskly went to the side of the inn, and stood below the Invisible Man's bedroom. He stood against the wall for a long time smoking his clay pipe, but his hands were trembling as he was too nervous. And he was constantly looking up at the window of the bedroom.

Meanwhile, in the bedroom Dr. Cuss and Reverend Bunting were still concentrating on the notebooks, when they suddenly felt something cold and hard being pushed at the back of their necks. They were shocked and horrified and tried to lift their heads to see what was happening. But the fireplace poker was pressed hard forcing their chins down and made them run out of breath.

Then they heard a cold whisper, "Don't move, you fools or I'll kill you both."

The reverend tried to look at the doctor's face only inches away from him and saw the same terror in the doctor's face as he himself was feeling.

"I didn't want to handle you in this way but I had no choice," said the Invisible Man. "Who gave you the right to investigate my room and go through my private diaries?"

Before they could say anything in reply their chins again hit the table, harder. "Where are my clothes? What have you done with my clothes you idiots?"

Pressing the two down on the table

"W-we don't know. We didn't see them. Please trust us. Mrs. Hall cleaned up the room before we came here," cried Dr. Cuss.

"I see. But I need clothes. And since mine are gone, I'll just have to-" And the Invisible Man whispered something into their ears.

"NO!" cried the doctor. "I can't do that!"

"How shameful!" protested Reverend Bunting.

"You've no choice and I'm really sorry for all this, my dear friends," said the Invisible Man sarcastically and made them sit up. Then he walked towards the window and opened it.

Across the road, outside the inn, Mr. Huxter, the tobacco shop owner was going for a walk when he suddenly saw the window of the bedroom being opened. Some moments later, he saw three thick books tied together with a pair of suspenders and a big bundle wrapped in blue tablecloth drop from the window and the tramp waiting there, grabbed them.

"Stop you thief!" shouted Mr. Huxter as he chased Marvel.

Huxter had gone only a few steps when he felt an invisible force grab his legs tightly. The next moment he was up in the air and then smashed into ground on his face, bloody and unconscious.

Hearing Huxter's cries of "Stop you thief!", all the customers sitting at the bar came outside. They wanted to chase the thief. Only Mrs. Hall stayed back in the bar to guard her cashbox.

Suddenly she heard the bedroom door open and was shocked to see the doctor running down the stairs only in his underwear, vest and jacket.

Huxter loses his clothes

"Stop him!" Don't let him escape!" he shouted. "He's got my trousers and all of Reverend's clothing!"

Just behind him came the reverend, helplessly trying to cover himself with the fireplace rug and the daily newspaper.

The two men joined the crowd in their awkward condition, to get their clothes back. Some tripped over Huxter's unconscious body and others were flung to the ground by a mysterious force and were stepped on. These violent attacks were enough to frighten the crowd to give up the chase and they returned back to their homes for safety.

The Invisible Man however, followed them back to Iping and destroyed anything he wanted, in his path. He destroyed Mr. Hall's cart at the inn, by chopping it into pieces, then he threw a streetlamp through the reverend's window in his parlor and a wheelbarrow through Mr. Huxter's shop window. Next, he went to Dr. Cuss's chamber and smashed each and every medicine bottle there. And finally, he tore off all the telegraph wires that connected Iping with the outside world.

Once that destruction was over, the Invisible Man left Iping. Nobody ever heard of him, or saw him or felt his presence in the village ever again.

FINDING AN ACCOMPLICE

By that evening, Thomas Marvel was far away from Iping. He wearily walked along the road, his arms loaded with three heavy books tied together and a bundle wrapped in a blue tablecloth. At every turn of the road, he eagerly looked for a chance to escape.

But the Invisible Man could sense what was going on in the tramp's mind and every now and then he beat down on Marvel's shoulders and warned him, "Don't even think of running away. For if you try, I swear I'll kill you."

"But I'm not trying to escape," protested the tramp and he was almost on the verge of crying. "I'm looking around because this place is new to me and I don't want to get lost!"

"It's bad that the villagers in Iping now know that I'm invisible. And those fools will inform the police and the newspapers to get me caught. Soon everyone will be looking for me everywhere. You mustn't leave me because I need you to do things for me."

"But I'm not strong. I'm weak. I would ruin all the plans that ye might make."

"Don't you dare! Don't even think of ruining my plans! I'm warning you," shouted the invisible voice. "Just follow my orders and you'll be safe and fine. I don't need the clothes any more so just throw the bundle away. But those books are more valuable than your life. Don't lose them!"

They walked whole night, and stopped for a few hours to take rest under some trees.

The next morning, they reached Port Stowe, the small seaside town. They waited for the bank to open and then while the roads were still empty, Marvel waited outside the bank and saw money flying out of the window and coming towards him through the air from inside the bank. He put them in the pockets of his coat and trousers and quickly moved away.

When he was far away from the bank, he panted hard. Fear and fatigue forced him to topple onto a bench outside a small inn. He put the books by his side.

Marvel waited outside the bank

After a few minutes an old seaman came out of the inn and settled himself beside him. The seaman just pretended to be reading the newspaper but he was actually curious about the thick books on the bench and the bulging pockets in Marvel's coat and trousers.

"Quite an interesting story," said the old seaman. "It says that an invisible man is moving around these parts."

"No!" shouted Marvel in shock. "Ye mustn't believe in stories like this. I don't!"

"Well, if the newspaper says it's true, then it must be true!"

"What do they say about his activities?"

"Everything! It says that it was found that he was invisible at a fight when bandages were torn off his head. And there was no head above his collar. Then he took off his clothes and fled. No one could track him after that."

The Invisible Man appears in the newspapers

"How shocking! And how could he manage to escape without any help from anyone? Does the newspaper say anything about any pal helping him?"

"No. But they think that he is in Port Stowe now. Just think man, if he's right beside you, thinking of robbing you, you would be able to do nothing to stop him because he's invisible. Neither can the police do a thing!"

When the seaman was talking, the tramp was looking around, listening for footsteps or any sound of movements to understand where the Invisible Man was. But he could hear nothing and felt safe. He thought this was his chance to escape. So he tilted his head towards the seaman and whispered, "Well, I know a little bit about this Invisible Man. And they are shocking things."

"Indeed! Please tell me!" cried the old seaman in excitement.

"The thing is," he began, "that I OW!" with that he moaned loudly in pain and put his hand over his left ear, which was bashed hard. Then as an explanation to his mysterious shout, he offered, "It's my tooth! It's paining' really bad. Got to go now." Then he picked up the books and ran away from the place.

"But what about the Invisible Man?" called the old seaman after him.

"Don't believe in that story. I know the fellow who convinced the newspapers to print that story."

"You stupid pot-bellied fellow, I thought you'd really know something about it! I just want to slap - "

But by then, Marvel was pulled along the road roughly and violently by an invisible force on his shoulder and arm.

Marvel is hounded by the Invisible Man

THE RAMPAGE AT JOLLY CRICKETER INN

Later that day, in a house on the outskirts of the nearby town of Port Burdock, a research scientist named Dr. Arthur Kemp was seated in his study, which was in the top floor of his house. The man was tall, thin and had blond hair and moustache. He looked up from his microscope during sunset, at the last bright rays that entered his room through the window.

He put down his pen, stood from his desk and stretched. He walked to the window and noticed some movement on the road. He saw a short, plump man running and waving his hands desperately, with difficulty. He was moving towards the town.

"Another idiot!" said Dr. Kemp to himself. "Running madly for no reason at all. Just like that fool who bumped into me this morning saying that, 'The Invisible man is here, sir! You better go back to your house!' It's simply difficult for me to understand how people can be so ignorant to believe in such nonsense!"

But the people in Port Burdock didn't think that it was nonsense. They saw the horror on Marvel's face and how he was perspiring as he was shouting warnings about the Invisible Man. They heard the heavy, wild footsteps just a few steps behind the tramp. They saw how a dog yelped

People ran in panic

because it was kicked hard by an invisible force. They saw an invisible arm elbowing apart two boys who were huddled together. They saw how a child was snatched from its mother and pushed to the side of the road by an invisible arm. They saw all that was happening and believed that there was indeed an Invisible Man.

People screamed and howled in panic, as they rushed towards their houses. Everywhere cries of "The Invisible Man has come," could be heard.

The people inside Jolly Cricketer Inn hadn't yet known about what was happening in the town, when suddenly the door opened violently and Thomas Marvel entered through it.

His hat was gone and his coat was torn in the neck but he was still holding those three books in his hands. He shut the door in terror, with his whole body against it and wept helplessly, “He’s here! He’ll kill me! The Invisible Man! For God’s sake, help me!”

“The stories in the newspaper are true then,” said the barman in shock.

“Quick! Lock the door!” shouted the policeman who was having a drink at the bar.

“Please save me!” cried the tramp. “I gave him the slip, but he’s chasing me. And I know he’ll kill me!”

Suddenly the door was banged wildly and it shook from top to bottom.

“He’s come!” shivered Marvel in horror, looking around for a place where he could hide himself. “Please save me. Don’ let him kill me!”

The barman hid the tramp behind the bar as the banging continued.

"Please save me!"

"For God's sake, don't open the door!" cried Marvel from his hiding place. "And lock all the doors to the inn. He's as cunning as the devil. He'll find any locked door."

"My God!" shuddered the barman. "There's the yard door and the kitchen door and the back..."

Just then they heard a door slammed. The barman ran towards the kitchen and returned with a large carving knife in his hands. "The kitchen door was locked but the yard door wasn't. He could be inside the house already!"

The policeman aimed his revolver at the door from the bar to the kitchen, as it suddenly burst open by itself. Suddenly Marvel was pulled out from behind the bar and was flung furiously across the room by an invisible force.

The policeman shot and the mirror behind the bar shattered and came smashing down to the floor.

The barman and the policeman froze in shock at the scene in front of them. Marvel was dragged out of the bar by invisible hands. He was taken to the kitchen and he was screaming hysterically.

The policeman recovered from the shock and rushed after Marvel before the door could be locked. He clutched the wrist that was dragging Marvel when suddenly he was punched hard and he fell down.

"I got him!" shouted the barman clawing at the air.

Finding himself free from the clutches of the Invisible Man, Marvel crawled between the legs of the fighting men. Then the Invisible Man screamed in pain as the policeman stamped hard on his foot.

But he recovered at once and attacked the policeman with his invisible fists and legs. The policeman crouched down on the ground in pain.

Marvel got hold of the thick books and swiftly crawled out of the room, unnoticed. He crawled to the kitchen and then ran towards the yard door.

Meanwhile, the policeman and the barman were puzzled and they found themselves struggling with emptiness.

"Where's he gone?" cried the barman.

"Must have gone out in the same way, just how he came in, through the yard door," said the policeman as he struggled to get up. "Let's go!"

As soon as they entered the kitchen, a plate swished by the policeman's head. "I'll teach him a lesson!" he barked as he pointed

A plate flew towards the policeman's head

his revolver towards the open yard door.

Five shots were fired and the bullets sped into the night outside the door. Then everything was silent.

"You must have shot him," said the barman. "I'll bring a lantern and we'll try to feel around for his body."

A MYSTERIOUS VISITOR

Dr. Kemp was totally engrossed in his research work, while the fight was going on at Jolly Cricketer Inn. He was concentrating on his microscope and notes, when suddenly he heard the gunshots from Port Burdock and he hurried to the window.

"What's the crowd there for, in front of the inn?" he muttered as he looked out at the town, “May be someone is drunk and is creating problems.”

Kemp returned to his desk and focused on his work for the next few hours, then suddenly his concentration was disturbed at the ring of the doorbell. He listened as the housekeeper went to answer it, but was surprised when she didn’t knock at his study to let him know about the visitor.

He waited for sometime and then went out of the room and called down, “Annie, who is at the door?”

“Nobody, sir. I think some naughty kid is playing pranks… ringing the bell and running off.”

Though Kemp returned to his work, he could not concentrate on his work as he kept thinking about it.

Finally, at two o’ clock in the morning, he

put down his pen and took a candle to light his way down to his bedroom. He was a scientist and with the indomitable curiocity of a scientist, he stopped to examine a dark spot on the floor at the foot of the stairs at the bedroom level.

He stooped down and touched the spot. "It's red and sticky and looks like drying blood. Perhaps Annie hurt herself. She'll probably clean it up in the morning."

He put the spot out of his mind and turned towards the bedroom. But he was shocked, when he saw a stain of blood at the handle of his door.

"Oh Lord!" he gasped in astonishment as he walked inside the room. "The bed spread and the sheets are drenched in blood and they are all ripped apart. And my pillow looks like someone slept on it! What's happening in here?"

The bed sheets were stained with blood

Just then a voice spoke in the room, "Thank Heavens! It's you Kemp!"

Kemp looked around the room but did not see anyone. Being a doctor and a scientist he certainly did not believe in ghosts or invisible voices.

Then he heard a sound near the washstand and spun around in surprise. He saw something hanging in midair and it looked like a blood-stained bandage wrapped around something that had the shape of an arm. But there was no arm! Kemp was about to touch the bandage when a voice spoke, just a few inches away from him.

"Don't be puzzled or frightened Kemp. I'm an invisible man."

Kemp stood there staring at the bandage, then stammered, "H-how can a b-bandage t-talk?

A-an in-invisible… m-man?"

"Yes that's right. An invisible man."

"Then what the people in this town have been discussing for so long is true!" blurted out Kemp, finding it really hard to believe what he was hearing. "I thought it was a stupid story made up, about some invisible man. But what's the bandage for?"

Kemp stepped forward to touch the bandage but his wrist was clutched by invisible fingers and was pushed back. The doctor was frightened at the creepy touch and turned pale. He tried to pull back his wrist but the grip tightened more. Desperate to free himself from the clutches of his enemy he began swinging his arms wildly in the air.

But his enemy was in full control of the situation and he took upperhand. Kemp was pushed hard and he fell on the bed. When he tried to shout for help, a corner of the sheet was stuffed inside his mouth and strong cold fingers tightened around his throat.

"You idiot! Try to reason!" shouted the Invisible Man, as Kemp struggled to free himself and fought violently, kicking and punching him. "Will you stop or do you want me to kill you?"

When Kemp finally stopped, the voice explained, "I'm really an Invisible Man. It's neither trick nor magic. Trust me, I want you to help me. I really don't want to hurt you, but if you go against me I'll have no other choice. You know me Kemp. I was your batchmate at the University College. My name is Jack Griffin. Do you remember me?

"Let me sit first. And then I'll be able to think," said Kemp.

Kemp was held down by the Invisible Man

The Invisible Man let him sit up.

"Are you the same Griffin to won the college medal for chemistry?" Kemp asked.

"Yes. You're right. It''s just that I've made myself invisible now."

"But believe me that's horrible! Why did you attempt to do something so devilish? And how did you-"

"Kemp please try to understand, I'm wounded and in a lot of pain. And tired and hungry too. Can I explain you later?"

Kemp stared in bewilderment, as he saw the blood stained bandage move across the room towards the chair. The seat went down a little as the Invisible Man sat on it.

"Can you get me something to drink?"

Kemp brought a glass of whiskey and moved towards the chair. "Where shall I give it to you?" he asked.

The chair screeched and Kemp felt the glass being taken out from his hand. The glass floated about twenty inches above the seat.

"Are you hypnotizing me?" asked Kemp.

"Don't talk like a fool!" shouted the voice. Then the glass tilted and whiskey poured out of it, creating a tiny pool in midair. "It's better if you listen to me without asking questions. I'm hungry and I need clothes too because the cold wind is freezing me. Is there a dressing gown?"

Kemp went to his cabinet and took out a long red robe, "How about this one?"

Invisible fingers snatched the robe from him. It fluttered strangely in midair, straightened out upright. Then the belt was knotted and it settled on the chair.

"Do you have some underwears, slippers and socks? And something to eat?"

The Invisible Man has a drink

"Sure," said Kemp moving towards the drawer to get the clothing that he was asked to provide by his visitor. "But this is so strange! I've never heard of anything like this till date!"

Still, Kemp went to the kitchen and brought some bread and meat. After coming back he saw that the Invisible Man was already wearing the underwear, socks and slippers.

"Well knives and forks? Never mind," said the voice as a slice of cold meat was taken from the plate. It stayed suspended in midair and bites from invisible teeth gnawed at it.

Kemp sat down on the edge of his bed still shaking his head in astonishment, "Invisible! That's really strange, man!"

"Actually what's really strange is that I was lucky enough to meet with you like this.

Food floating through mid-air

After all, you can bandage my wound properly. Though my blood is invisible you'll be able to see once it starts forming clots. So you can well see where I was wounded."

"And how did you get wounded?"

"Because of that foolish tramp... Marvel! He was supposed to help me but that fool ran away with my notebooks and money instead."

"Did he shoot you? I think I heard the shots from the town."

"No, some fool at the inn shot me... But it's enough for now Kemp. Get me a cigar to finish off this meal."

Kemp got a cigar and stared in shock as the smoke traveled through the Invisible Man's mouth, down his throat and out of his nostrils. "You must tell me in detail how did you make this possible. I'm too eager to know."

Having a smoke

"Kemp can't you see how exhausted I am and how painful this wound is?" the voice suddenly groaned, and the robe leaned forward with sleeves upwards, to support an invisible head with invisible hands. "Oh Lord! Kemp I haven't slept for three days and three nights, as I was constantly moving from one place to another."

"You can sleep now. Sleep here in my bedroom."

"No I can't sleep! Marvel will escape if I sleep. And then the police might also find me."

Kemp exclaimed in shock, "Police?"

The Invisible Man banged his invisible fist on the table. "I'm a fool Kemp!" he exclaimed. "Here I'm sitting in your house and I can't even trust you!"

"Of course you can trust me. I'l never let out any secret that you might tell me, I promise. Nobody will know that you're here, in my house. You can lock yourself in this room and I can assure you that nobody would disturb you."

"All right then," said the voice with a yawn. "I'm too tired and I accept your offer of this room. But I'm sorry I can't talk more tonight. But I'll assure you that this invisibility is possible. I thought of not telling this to anyone but now I see that I must have a partner. We can do a lot of amazing things together. But I'll explain tomorrow. Now if I don't sleep, I'l surely die."

"Good-night then!" said Kemp as he shook an invisible hand.

His visitor followed him to the door and then warned him, "Don't even try to interfere with my plans or get me arrested. It'll not be good for you!"

AN AMAZING DISCOVERY

As the door shut behind him violently and the key was turned in the lock, Dr. Kemp slapped his forehead with his hand and muttered to himself, "Was that a dream? Has everyone in this world gone mad... or have I? Or am I imagining things?" Then he felt the bruises in his neck where invisible fingers had held him during the struggle. "No, this can't be a dream or an imagination. It's a fact, and it's not possible to deny."

Just after that Kemp went downstairs into his small chamber, where patients visited him for check-ups. But his practice of medicine was mostly done through research. He lit up the gas lamp and picked up the daily newspaper that his housekeeper had left for him at the desk.

He read each article intensely, bewildered at the headlines which said, "Strange Case in Iping" and "Entire Village in Sussex Becomes Crazy". As he read he came to know of the weird incidents caused by the invisible man, who harmed and injured people, attacked a constable, harassed a doctor and a reverend and spread terrors everywhere.

When he finished reading all the news about the Invisible Man, he slumped down in his chair, wondering, "But why did he chase the tramp called Thomas Marvel? These

Unable to decide

stories don't talk about any accomplice. After learning about him from these stories I'm convinced that he's not only invisible but also a lunatic. He's mad enough to murder people!"

Dr. Kemp was awake for the rest of the night, pacing up and down in his office, thinking about what he should do. When his housekeeper knocked in the morning, he was still in his office and asked her to serve breakfast for two, in his study upstairs but asked her to stay back downstairs on the ground floor.

Kemp stayed in his office till the morning newspaper came, which had an account of the happenings at the Jolly Cricketer Inn the night before. Thomas Marvel was also mentioned in the newspaper and it quoted him as saying, "The Invisible Man forced me to stay with him for twenty-four hours."

However Marvel did not mention about the three books and the money that he was carrying with him.

"This is pretty frightening and I don't know what the man might do," he muttered. "He's a lunatic and he's here in my house as thin and free as the air. What do I do?... Would I be breaking my word if I...?"

Kemp thought for sometime and then took a decision. He sat at his desk and wrote a brief letter. He put it in an envelope, sealed it and addressed it to "Colonel Adye, Port Burdock Police."

Just as Kemp was handing the letter to his housekeeper to deliver to town, a horrific noise came from his bedroom. Something was rushing across the room with violent speed, chairs were flung and broken, and the washstand and glasses were shattered and smashed into pieces.

Kemp writes a brief note

Kemp whispered, "Quick!" to the housekeeper and rushed upstairs.

The bedroom door was till locked from the night before, but it was opened immediately when Kemp knocked loudly.

"What's wrong?" he asked the headless robe. "Why are you smashing things?"

"Nothing," said the voice above the robe. "I just got angry. I forgot that this arm was injured, when I went to use it."

"It seems that you have these fits of temper every now and then," said Kemp as he stooped down to pick up the pieces of the broken glass and organized the overturned furniture.

After finishing, he looked at the emptiness above the robe and said, "The papers are full with news about you and all the incidents that occurred at Iping and Port

Burdock. Everyone is trying to find out where you are, but of course, you're safe here as nobody knows that you're with me and I'm going to help you."

The Invisible Man started pacing up and down the room and sweared under his breath. He stopped when Kemp asked him for breakfast and followed the doctor upstairs to his study.

Kemp glanced nervously out of the window and he had a strange feeling when he saw a headless, handless robe sitting opposite to him, at the table.

He watched in amazement as invisible hands took the napkin and placed it in the lap of the robe.

"I must know about this invisibility of yours, Griffin," said Kemp. "It's obvious that I'm truly amazed at your wonderful

Clothes with no one in them

discovery and I'm curious to know all about it."

"Wonderful, yes it was at the beginning. But now I've doubts... and I can't be sure unless we can do phenomenal things with this invisibility. Now I'll tell you what I've been through."

THE INVISIBLE MAN TELLS HIS STORY

"Perhaps you didn't know that at the age of twenty-two, I switched my studies from medicine to physics. The study of light and its relationship to solids and liquids intrigued me. How interestingly a piece of glass becomes practically invisible in water, when light passes through it."

"Yes of course! But human being is not transparent like glass," said Kemp. "So what relation does this have with your invisibility?"

"Ah Kemp! A human being is transparent. He's, as a matter of fact more transparent. Every part of his body--his flesh, bones, hair, nerves except the red blood cells and certain pigments, or coloring matters are made up of nothing other than transparent, colorless tissue. For six long years I worked wholeheartedly on these theories but didn't tell a soul or publish my findings until everything was perfect. I wrote every detail of my research, every formula I invented, and everything else that made my experiment successful, in my three notebooks, which the tramp has stolen for me. That's the reason why I must find him or they will be lost forever."

"But how did you make the blood and pigments invisible?"

"That took another three years. And Kemp, I almost had to give up my research because I didn't have enough money to continue with it. But I was determined not to stop and stole money from my father. But unfortunately the money wasn't my father's and he committed suicide by shooting himself." The Invisible Man sighed deeply and got up from the table.

He went and stood by the window and Kemp stared at the headless figure for a few minutes without speaking. Then a sudden thought crossed his mind. He got up and held the invisible wrist and let the Invisible Man back to the chair.

"You're too exhausted, my friend. I don't think you should move around like this. Please sit down and take rest. And go ahead with the story."

Kemp sat down between the Invisible Man's chair and the window, blocking the view of the road to town.

He went on. "The money I stole was enough to buy all the equipments I needed to carry on with the experiment. At first, I made a piece of white wool fabric invisible. Oh what a strange feeling it was Kemp, to put my hand into emptiness and yet feel the solidarity of the fabric. But I had trouble finding it when I threw it on the floor."

"Incredible!" cried Kemp.

"Very soon I found my next experiment. And Kemp believe me this experiment was even more amazing. It was the straving neighborhood cat that stayed in my lab."

"And could you make the cat invisible too?"

"Yes. Almost. I mixed the drugs I had developed with some food and laid her down on a pillow. She was unconscious for several hours while every part of her body became

Feeding a cat

invisible, except the green pigment at the back of her eyes. Those pigments were visible when she awoke. I saw her for the last time with only those two pigments, before she jumped out of the window.

"The experiment was successful and I became more enthusiastic than ever. My brain was on fire and I dreamt of all the amazing things that an invisible man could do. There was no backing off from the experiment, but my money had almost finished. I couldn't pay the rent to my landlord. The very thought of making myself invisible to the world and disappearing, raised the hairs on my arms and I felt nothing could stop me from making the experiment successful. So I started making plans."

"That day itself, I packed my three notebooks and mailed them to myself at a package pick-up office on the other side of London. Then I came back, mixed the drugs and drank the potion."

"I sat there waiting to see the result, when there was a loud banging at my door. I woke up and realized that I was in a sick, drowsy state. I opened the door to find the landlord who came to handover the eviction notice to me. But as he looked at me, he let out a sharp cry, dropped the notice and ran down the hall, shuddering. I was surprised and after locking the door, hurriedly went to the mirror. And then I understood why he was scared. It was because my face had turned as white as snow!

"I can't describe in words Kemp, what kind of suffering I went through that night. The very thought of it horrifies me even today. It felt as if my body was burning. I was sick to my stomach. I became unconscious

The horrible experience

several times and then again came back to my senses. This continued throughout the night and I wept and groaned and talked to myself. I wanted to die, but I wanted to live also.

"By morning the pain had stopped. Lying on my bed I brought my hands near my eyes and saw that they looked like clouded glass. As the day wore, they became clearer and thinner until I could see the room through them. The same happened with my arms and legs and then my bones and blood."

"By evening I was struggling to get up from bed. It was almost like being a baby again, just learning to walk, for I was stepping on legs that were invisible to my own eyes. In the mirror also I couldn't see my reflection."

"I was so happy Kemp, but just then there was a violent banging at my door and the angry voice of my landlord threatened, if I didn't open the door then he and his son would break into my room. When I didn't reply, he began attacking the door with axes."

"Kemp, I was desperate! I didn't want them to know about the chemicals or the equipments that I had been using for the experiment. So I gathered them, piled up a heap of rubbish and papers on them and then turned on the gas. As I headed for the window, I threw a match onto the pile and bid goodbye to all the things I owned."

"What! You mean you set the entire house on fire and risked others lives?"

"What else could I do?" barked the Invisible Man. "It was the only way to protect my secret. As I saw the house burning, from a distance I thought of all the wild and amazing things that I could do now, without getting caught. And I was thrilled!"

"Where did you go then?"

"First I went to the package pick-up office to collect my books. And how funny it was to slap people on my way, or flinging their hats off their heads or snatching packages from women's arms or swinging baby carriages around in circles! Everyone was so startled because they failed to understand what was happening and I was amused!

"But I soon found myself bumping into deliverymen, the passing horses kicked me and the afternoon crowd almost crushed me. Dogs couldn't see me but followed me sniffing, because of their extraordinary sense of smell. Besides, my bare feet was already sore from the rocks and hard mud on the road and blood dripped from them. And there was one more problem. I was naked and the cold January wind froze me and left me trembling. It didn't occur to me that my invisible body would be affected by the weather."

Dogs were able to smell him out

"And then small boys caused another big problem. As I quickly walked, two of them noticed my footprints in the road and were too curious.

'Look!' said one of them. 'There are footprints, but no man!'

" 'And see there is also blood in one of the footprint,' said the other.

"I began to run but they followed me shouting, 'Feet! Running feet!'

"Soon a crowd started running after the two boys. I managed to stay ahead of them all for several blocks, until I found a dry stretch of road. I stopped, dried my muddy feet and then continued walking leaving no traces behind my pursuers to follow."

Hearing the word "pursuers", Dr. Kemp glanced quickly out of the window, and at the same time urged the Invisible Man to go on with the story, "Carry on Griffin. What happened after that?"

Trying to enter the department store

A THREAT

The story continued. "There looked to be a greater threat of snowfall that night. You could make that out from the colour of the sky. I realised that my game would be up if the flakes would come along and settle on me. I was in dire need to find some nice and warm place, where I could collect my wits and think of my future plans."

"I couldn't devise any means of going

inside locked houses and I couldn't even take the risk of opening inn doors and allow my invisible body to attract any attention. However, when I suddenly found myself standing before the Omnium departmental store, I realised that this was the perfect place where I could go in and solve my problems of food, clothing and money."

"I kept standing there for a long time and then my opportunity came. I waited for the doorman to open the door for a customer and in the process, managed to smuggle myself in with her. I loitered inside the store, and soon reached a warm corner, where I found a pile of mattresses. I took refuge there for quite some time and formulated my plans. I waited for the store to close, so that I could find some food, collect the clothing that I would need for myself, obtain the necessary cash from the store's register, sleep like a log on the store beds and then leave the next day and gather all the note books that I needed."

"So what happened? Were you able to do all that?"

"No, not exactly in the way that I had planned it. I managed to find the food, clothing and money that I needed and I had then fallen asleep on the store's mattresses. However, the problem appeared when the store opened when I was still awake. I was immediately spotted and therefore I got up and started to run amongst shocked salesmen. I ran along an aisle and shot through another, a headless figure wearing trousers, coat, gloves, shoes and hat. I realised that if I were to make my escape, I would have to take of all my clothes. I jumped behind a counter and tore them all off my body."

"Did they find you?" Kemp broke in.

Running amongst shocked salesmen

"Of course not! I was able to run off from there before the police could arrive. But then there was something else that was bothering me now ... I had no clothes and I had no money. And I couldn't even run with the food as people would be able to see that in my stomach until and unless it would digest it completely."

"That never crossed my mind... But what about the snow? Did that not bother you?"

"Not really ... The snow had already melted by then. But then, I did get aware about the other threats issued by weather. Rain was perhaps one of the most harmful, because it left a watery outline, as if I were a bubble and I also figured out that fog would also do me the same harm. Therefore, you can imagine that my real problem was not the snow, but rather I was affected by the strong, icy winds that were blowing that day.

I just had to find some clothing, and that too rather fast. I could sense a cold flowing in and therefore I had to carefully prevent myself from sneezing, in order to protect my invisibility."

"But soon my luck improved as I came towards a small costume shop on a lonely street. Luckily no one saw me open the door. I guess the owner was sitting somewhere at the back, where he was busy eating his lunch. I presume he had very sharp ears, because the minute I came in, he turned around to face me. Obviously when he saw that there was nobody there, he turned back and resumed his earlier activity... Or at least that is what I thought."

"I positioned myself in the front of a clothes rack and was busy looking at the clothes there, when suddenly I heard this man approaching me from the back. This time I found him carrying a revolver and swinging it in all directions, saying, 'Come out, come out, whoever you are …' He obviously was not going to wait for me to even think about giving myself up and consequently fired several shots… You wouldn't believe it, but one of those shots missed me by just a few inches. It was that close. I was obviously rather scared, but then … I took care of him."

"What? Don't tell me you killed him …"

"I don't think that blow on the back of his head was strong enough to kill him. No, I don't think that I killed him. Come on now, Kemp … do you think I am going to stoop down to become a murderer? I had no other option then. He had a gun and I could in no way let him describe my appearance …"

"But that man was in his own house and you had gone in with the intention of robbing him!"

Trying to run away

"So, you want to blame me for that, do you? Come on Kemp, tell me what other opinion have you made about me?"

Kemp breathed slowly and immediately changed his stance. He shook his head slowly and said, "Yes, I guess you are right! There was nothing that you could have done. Carry on … What happened next?"

"I took care of all my clothing needs immediately. I also obtained for myself some dark glasses, a wig and also some whiskers. Needless to say I helped myself to all the silver shillings and gold sovereigns that he had. It was most essential that I do that. With that I was now ready to once again move out."

"And that man? What about him? You left him all tied up inside?" asked Kemp.

"Oh that was hardly anything. He must have managed to kick himself out of that mess soon. Coming back to myself, I was starving at that point. Therefore I just had to go and eat something. However the problem remained that I couldn't go into any public place, without the chances of causing some alarm. So I finally went to an eating joint where there were private dining areas. I explained that as I was badly disfigured I preferred to eat alone."

The Invisible Man turned towards the window, where Kemp was moving to and fro.

In order to keep his guest talking, Kemp put in, "Iping? Did you go there after that?"

"Absolutely! I had already sent across my books, my clothing and all my equipment. I had a plan of working there completely undisturbed, with the only hope – something that I still do have – of adopting the formula by which I can again gain my visibility. But no yet Kemp, not yet! I will apply that formula on to myself only when I want to. And therefore, you can imagine, I have a lot of things to do before I am once again visible. It is for that Kemp that I strongly need your help."

"Come on now, you don't expect me to help you attack people like you did in Iping!"

"Don't worry too much about them Kemp! They'll recover sooner than you think. However, Thomas Marvel will have a bad time, once I catch up with him. He'll pay for what he did to me. And anybody else who tries to interfere with my plans will also have to pay the same price. With my bare hands, Kemp ... With my bare hands ... I'll kill them all."

Thomas Marvel will pay the price

MR. KEMP'S VISITOR ESCAPES

"I just read in the newspapers, he is behind the bars and he himself requested the police to put him in the strongest of jails."

"Ha ha ha! But that's not going to stop me from getting him..."

His wild laughter silenced the opening of the door in the front. "Don't worry Kemp! We shall establish our rule of terror in a much planned manner. For instance, we'll conquer your place, Burdock and then unleash terror on it. Whoever goes against us will end up paying the maximum price for it DEATH!

We shall kill everyone and anyone who'd try to hamper our plans!"

Kemp tried to but in, "you must understand... that I can't...,"

"Quiet! I hear footsteps... Someone's here."

"Just your imagination," continued Kemp. "I can't be a part of this plan of yours. I propose, on the other hand, that you publish your experiments. You must gain more coverage of the state that you are in. May be then, someone can help..."

"I heard someone coming up the stairs. Did you betray me?"

"What are you saying?"

"For your sake, I hope you haven't," cried Griffin as he moved towards the door.

Dr Kemp stops him

Before he could move forward, Kemp came in between and tried to push him away from the door.

"So... My worst fears have come true. I have been betrayed."

He immediately began untying his dressing gown and throwing away all his clothes.

Having no other alternative at that time, Kemp threw the door open. The Invisible Man immediately sprang upon him.

Kemp immediately pushed the Man inside and tried to turn the lock. But the key slipped from his hand before he could lock the door. Kemp trembled with fear. The door handle was the only thing he could attempt to yank. But even before he could pull the door, Griffin came in between.

Before Kemp could react, he felt strong

Running away once again

invisible fingers clutch his throat. He therefore, had to let go of the handle and defend himself. The gown started pushing Kemp towards the corner of the stairs at the top.

Colonel Adye, who was coming up the stairs at that time, was completely out of his wits at what he saw before him. Moments later, he could see the dressing gown jump on Dr. Kemp; fingers that could not be seen were trying to grab his throat. Griffin then shoved himself into his belly. Then, suddenly the dressing gown tried to run down the stairs.

Two more police officers, who were following Adye up the stairs, took cover behind their superior. They just heard the front door shut behind them.

A bloody and tattered Kemp turned towards the door. He knew that there was no point in going after him. It was too late.

AN ATTEMPT TO TRACE THE INVISIBLE MAN

After quite some time Kemp came back to his senses. He led Colonel Adye into his office, where they sat over their drinks.

"He's a lunatic!" cried the Doctor, "He has completely lost his humanity. He has terrorized everyone and is all set to harm people for his selfish schemes. He even plans to kill people...and he'll get away with it too unless he is stopped."

"But he has to be caught," exclaimed Adye.

"You have to hurry up then... and catch him while he is still in this district. Once he's out of the countryside, he'll kill anybody who gets in his way. He was talking about some rule of terror and that too here in Port Burdock. Put in your forces at stations, roads and ports. Even try calling in the Army. The only reason I foresee his staying in this place, is to get his notebooks from Marvel."

"I understand...that tramp in jail."

"I would suggest you stop Griffin from sleeping and eating. Ban all houses, shop and even inns, so that he can't find any accommodation. Let's hope that there are cold nights and also heavy rains. That would display his outline. And then we would be able to capture him. If we don't do something Colonel, I shudder to think what's in store for us."

Making plans to catch the Invisible Man

"Doctor, I strongly suggest that you come along and help us to search for this guy," advised Adye.

With Kemp's consent, they set off for the police station. "Dogs! Get dogs...they should be able to pick up his scent," said Kemp.

"I'l contact the guy who raises and trains bloodhounds. Anything more that you can suggest?"

"I remember him telling me that his food remains visible till it is digested. So he'll have to hide after that. Order your men to comb the shrubs around here, and make sure that they don't carry their guns. He obviously can't keep one, but he definitely can use one."

"And what else?"

"Cut glass...spread that on the roads as well, so that his feet get cut. I know that it's a rather devilish thought, but believe me, it's nothing in comparison to what he plans to do. We just have to outsmart him."

Within some time, news spread through the countryside like wildfire, that there was an Invisible Man roaming about, and had to be captured-dead or alive! A special police force was deployed to go to people's houses and warn them to stay indoors and properly secure their houses. Schools were shut down. Warning posters were attached to all nearby lamp-posts that were there. The police also sent telegraphic messages to all enforcement agencies across the country. Within minutes of this circulation, there were men everywhere with guns, clubs and even bloodhounds, waiting to capture the Invisible Man.

However, even with all these precautions, the dead body of a certain Lionel Wicksteed was found. He was a middle aged man, who served as a caretaker. Why was he targeted & clubbed to death by an iron rod will perhaps never be known. The police located the blood-stained iron bar right next to the man. The forces even gave him the benefit of the doubt have been using that iron bar as a measure for defense. They decided that Wicksteed must have followed the iron bar out of curiosity, wondering why it had been floating around in the air.

Very soon news about the Invisible Man was coming in through the whole countryside. There came in reports from a farm at Hintondean, located at quite a distance from Port Burdock. They contained the fact that there had been some voices wailing, coughing and making many more audible sounds all across the field.

On hearing this information, Adye turned

The Invisible Man hiding in the countryside

towards Kemp & informed him, "I guess the culprit must have understood that you had passed on all this information to us, and that we are desperately trying to get him caught. He must have also noticed all the posters that have been put up and all the extra police forces patrolling the areas."

"Yes, but you don't have an idea what a desperate, intelligent, lunatic can do..." sighed Kemp.

As Kemp claimed, the Invisible Man woke up that morning with renewed vigor and determination. He was also full of hatred and with this he was also set to fight his last war with mankind, a fight that he was absolutely confident of winning.

THE ASSAULT AT KEMP'S HOUSE

Next morning, Dr. Kemp found that he had received a mail from Hintondean. He was busy having his lunch, when the mail was placed before him. He found a rather greasy paper and the message was written in pencil

"Citizens of Port Burdock,

I must admit that you have shown amazing wit, yet the objective of the same still eludes me. You've denied me from even the slightest comforts that a human being is in need of food and sleep. However you are not successful as I have done both.

And let me tell you that Port Burdock is no longer ruled by the Queen of England, but by me... The Invisible Man! Please inform this to everyone.

Just to let you all know about my power, I shall begin my reign with the execution of a man called Kemp. He may hide himself wherever he wants to, lock as many locks as he may want, or hide under as many covers as he wants I shall kill him today. Whoever tries to save him shall be my next target. Today's the end of Kemp!"

Kemp jumped up with fear and instructed that all doors, windows and shutters were securely fastened. Leaving nothing to

The assault at Kemp's house

chance, he even brought out his revolver. He filled the ammunition and in a crazy state went back to complete his lunch.

Then all of a sudden he banged his fists on the table and screamed, “I’ve decided that I will be the bait and then we shall capture him.”

He immediately wrote a letter and ran to give it to his innkeeper. He ordered her to rush with the letter to Colonel Adye, “I’m being tracked by a madman. It is essential to give this letter to the Colonel.”

Within a few minutes Kemp heard a knock on his door. He opened the door but kept the safety chain, so that he could protect himself from getting attacked. He immediately heard Colonel Adye's voice. “It’s me Dr Kemp! There's been trouble ... your housekeeper's been taken down!”

"Oh, my goodness! How is she?"

"We've brought her to the station. She thinks that she has seen a ghost. Says she was carrying a letter from you to me, when it was snatched out of her hands.

"Good Lord! Why didn't that cross my mind? He'd take only an hour to get here from Hintondeon. He must have already reached."

Colonel Adye looked bewildered. "What are you saying? I can't make a word of it!"

Kemp immediately handed him the letter that he had received from Griffin. Adye read it quickly.

"He won't make the mistake of coming here. That's for sure."

"No, I strongly..."

There was a sound of a crash upstairs. Both men ran towards the stairs. "Quick, someone's in my study."

Once inside the room, the men found the broken pieces from all three windows, scattered all over.

"He's started," panicked Kemp.

Adye looked suspicious. "How did he get up here? We're on the third floor."

"I don't know... all that."

Again there was a shattering sound from the bedroom downstairs. "He's trying to destroy the whole house. But little does he understand, with the inside shutters secured, the glass will just break and fall on him. He'll get cut."

As this ordeal progressed, Adye told Kemp, "Hand me your revolver, I'll go and get the bloodhounds. You just secure yourself within the house."

Kemp quickly led Adye towards the door. The minute Adye slipped out, Kemp

Colonel Adye walks boldly down the steps

slammed the door shut and breathed a sigh of relief.

The Colonel made across the steps to the lawns in firm, loud step. Nearing the gate, he could feel a gentle wind blow through the grass. Suddenly a voice called out towards him, “Halt.”

Adye put forward all his courage and roared, “Who are you?”

“Go back into the house.”

“I have to attend to some work.”

“What work?”

“That is none of your business.”

Just as he completed his sentence, a hand gripped his neck and threw him a sharp kick around his legs. Adye stumbled to the ground. Just as he was trying to reach for the revolver, he got a sharp blow on his face and the revolver was taken away from his hands.

Adye saw the revolver, suspended in mid air. The voice spoke again, "I have nothing against you, but I have to stop you from going into town and getting the force. Come on - start moving back to the house."

"I don't suppose Dr. Kemp will open the door anymore."

"That's a chance that you have to take."

"Please, please do not kill him."

"I guarantee nothing!" So saying the Invisible Man pushed Adye with his revolver.

Meanwhile, staring at the strange display of events outside, Kemp could not understand why Adye was not shooting. But the minute he saw Adye move towards the house, followed by a hanging revolver, everything was clear to him.

But suddenly Kemp saw Adye jump at the

revolver. But he barely missed it. Then there was scuffle, which stopped only at a bang, with thick, blue smoke rising. He saw Adye stagger back and cling on to his chest. And then he lay down on the floor, dead.

Kemp could not even move a muscle. He kept staring at the sight outside. He could see the revolver vanish, as two policemen came charging towards the house.

Suddenly the silence was broken by the sound of his bell ringing hurriedly. Kemp got tremendously nervous as he moved towards the door. He opened it with the safety chain secure.

Suddenly he heard that someone was trying to strike the kitchen door with an axe. Kemp looked back to the door and found two policemen standing there. He let them in and screamed, "He's here and he's armed with a revolver and an axe."

Breaking through the kitchen window

The sounds from the kitchen stopped and Kemp realized that the Invisible Man has entered inside the house now.

He rushed with the policemen towards the dining room, where he armed them with the fireplace pokers. Suddenly the revolver and the axe were seen, dangling in mid-air.

The policemen swung their pokers to stop a blow from the axe, but a shot was fired. In their second attempt, they managed to shake the revolver away from the hand.

The Invisible Man dropped down his axe and looked towards the policemen. "Get out of the way. It is Kemp that I want."

"But it is you that we want," yelled the policeman, waving their pokers towards the axe.

The axe took its time, but suddenly came towards one of them and struck him heavily on his helmet, completely bashing him.

The second policeman pointed his poker towards the axe; there was a sharp cry of pain as the axe dropped to the floor. He again swung his poker, but this time he missed. He kept moving his poker, but there was no more contact.

Meanwhile, the first policeman had got around. He sat upon the floor - his face covered with flood and asked, "Where is he"?

"I hit him once... But it seems that he's not here anymore. He must have escaped. There! Look, that window is open. Looks like our hero, the Doctor must have escaped through that, with the Invisible Man running behind him."

THE END OF TERROR

Meanwhile, Dr. Kemp crossed the vegetable garden, followed by the imprints of footsteps on the grass. He violently banged on the door of his neighbor, but that was of no help. They refused to open the door because of the Invisible Man.

Kemp quickly thought about what to do in that situation and consequently ran towards the town. He carefully ran over rough ground

Asking the neighbours for help

and also over the scattered pieces of broken glass. He had calculated the injuries that would be inflicted on the pair of bare feet following him.

As the town port came within his view, he could feel the breaths of the Invisible Man on his back.

"He's chasing! The Invisible Man is after me..."

That immediately dispersed the crowd that had gathered there. Women moved into the nearby houses with their children, as a few road-workers standing there, rushed towards the Doctor with their tools.

Seeing that movement, Kemp stopped and screamed, "A circle"

Before he could complete his sentence, he was hit by a sharp punch in his ears. He lost balance temporarily, but just as he managed to steady himself, he defended himself by throwing his fist towards his unseen adversary. He missed his mark, but was hit below the jaw and that sent him flying through the ground. He could feel the force of a knee dig into his chest, and fingers wrap around his neck.

Kemp turned on his back and tried to free himself from the hold. He just managed to grip the hand, when a swinging spade from one of the workmen managed to hit something. Immediately the grip loosened from the doctor's neck and he could feel a weight drop on his body.

Kemp wriggled out of that posture and reversed him, pinning a space to the ground.

"He's here," yelled Kemp, "Come on, grab his feet, and secure him to the ground."

Soon there were men falling all around

Kemp, building a huge human pile from the ground. A weak voice mumbled from below, "Spare me! Please spare me..."

"Move back! Get away!" protested Kemp. "I think he is hurt."

The men obeyed his orders, and Kemp sat up trying to feel the hands of the Invisible Man.

"It's just a trick. Don't let him go," yelled one of the men.

"No. He's really hurt," screamed back Kemp.

"I think that's blood on his face." The Doctor drew his hands over the Invisible Man's chest, to feel a heartbeat. "I can't feel anything. I think it's all over."

"Good heavens! Look at that..." screamed a woman from the crowd.

As people traced the direction in which

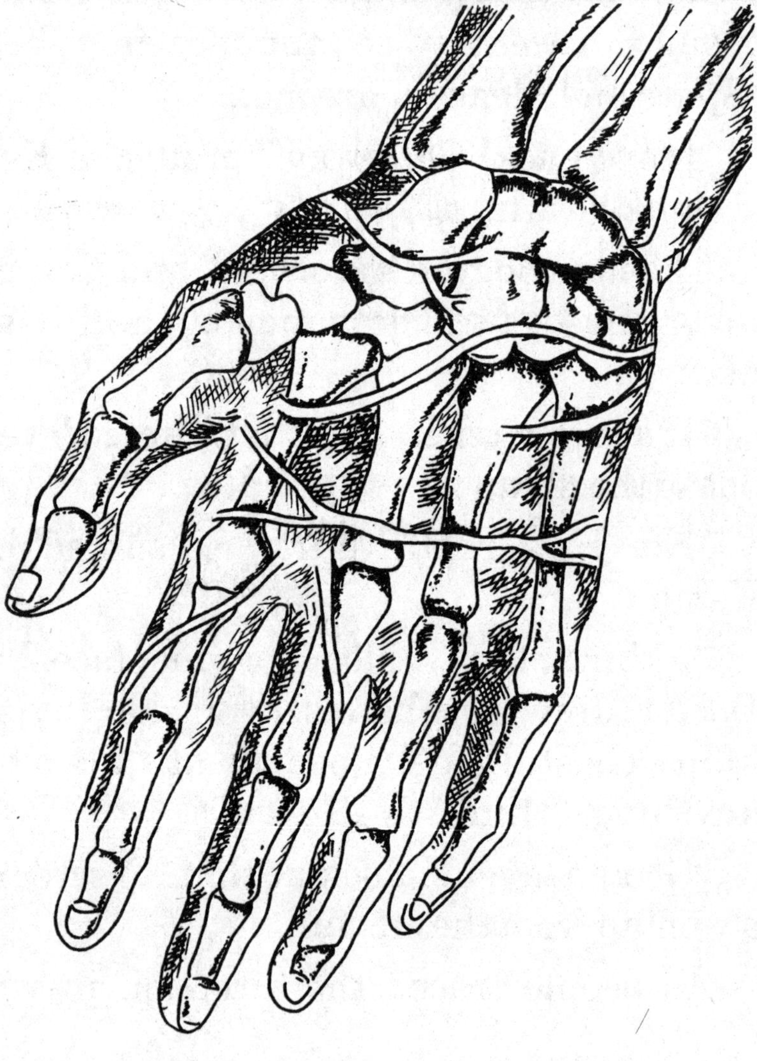

A hand of glass

her fingers were pointed, a cloudy hand had appeared - all complete with veins, arteries, nerves and even bones. As people stared at that in total disbelief, the hand kept changing from transparent to translucent.

"He's coming back! His feet are showing too," exclaimed another man.

Slowly and steadily, the whole body was becoming visible.

Kemp immediately took off his jacket to cover the dead body of the thirty-year-old Jack Griffin, the erstwhile Invisible Man.

"His face, cover his face as well," yelled a lady from the crowd.

Soon someone brought some cloth and carried it over Griffin's face. Having nothing left to do, Kemp carried the dead body of his batch mate into the inn.

THE INVISIBLE MAN INN

The saga of the Invisible Man has come to an end now. However, if you're interested in hearing more about him, find your way to The Invisible Man Inn near about Port Stove. You shall find there a short, plump man, the prosperous innkeeper. His name is Thomas Marvel.

If you buy some food from him ensuring his profit, you'll get to hear long tales about the Invisible Man.

However, if asked about the three notebooks and he will tell you that those were hidden by the Invisible Man himself- and that Dr. Kemp had falsely accused him, of stealing them.

But on Sundays, when the inn remains closed, Marvel locks himself in his parlor and from the cupboard takes out a box. Inside the box three notebooks are hidden.

He flips through the pages and goes through all the coded massages recorded in them.

So "Someday...someday I will get through shall...obviously not repeat what he did."

Kemp & Adye had questioned Thomas Marvel many times about the three notebooks but he will never let go of them, till the time he is alive.

Marvel recounts his stories.